ANCIENT (

BY

Stephan Weaver

© 2015 Copyright

No part of this book may be reproduced in any form or by any electronic or mechanical means including information storage and retrieval systems, without permission in writing from the author.

Contents

Introduction

CHAPTER I: The Rise of Ancient Greece

CHAPTER II: Archaic Greece

CHAPTER III: Classical Greece

CHAPTER IV: Hellenistic Greece

CHAPTER V: The Fall of Ancient Greece

Bonus Chapter: 10 Little Known Facts about Ancient Greece

Introduction

From 800 BC to 30 BC, Ancient Greece remained a powerful entity, playing a significant role in sculpting the world we live in today. The era saw the rise of innovative thinking, artistry, literature and much besides.

Chronicling the fascinating periods of Ancient Greece, this eBook gives you a lofty insight into histories most fascinating era.

From Archaic Greece to the rise and fall of Alexander the Great; from the Hellenistic era to the demise of Ancient Greece and the conquest of Rome—this eBook will give you a breath taking account of each epoch.

CHAPTER I

The Rise of Ancient Greece

The era of Ancient Greece lasted from the Archaic period (800 BC- 500 BC) to the end of antiquity (600 AD). Ancient Greece includes the Classical period, which flourished from 500- 323 BC, and the Hellenistic period, which commences with Alexander the Great's death and ends with the invasion of the Roman Republic.

Early History of Greece

During the Paleolithic era there were already settlements and agricultural practices that had begun in Greece; this is proved by the discoveries at the Petralona and Franchthi caves— two of the world's earliest human occupations.

Neolithic Age— 6000-2900 BC

During the **Neolithic Age** (6000- 2900 BC) in Greece, there were permanent settlements (mainly in the north of Greece), domestication of animals and advancement of agriculture. Archeological discoveries in the northern region of Greece illustrate that there was a migration from Anatolia. This is evidenced by the ceramic cups and bowls and figures discovered there; these artifacts share similar qualities peculiar to the Neolithic finds in Anatolia. The settlers were mainly farmers and dwelled in single-room houses built out of stone.

Cycladic Civilization— 3200- 1100

The **Cycladic Civilization** (3200-1100 BC) thrived in Aegean Sea (Delos, Naxos and Paros). This civilization gives one of the first finds of recurrent human occupation in the area. In the era of the Cyclades, the habitants were accustomed to fishing and trade; the temples and houses of the time were constructed of finished stone. This era is commonly split into three phases: Early Cycladic, Middle Cycladic and Late Cycladic. The two latter phases overlapped and finally merged with the Minoan Civilization, and the disparity between two phases became indistinguishable.

Minoan Civilization— 2700- 1500 BC

The **Minoan Civilization** (2700- 1500 BC) thrived in Crete, quickly becoming the superpower of the sea in the region. The archaeologist Sir Arthur Evans coined the word 'Minoan' after the ancient King Minos of Crete. It was in 1900 BC that the archeologist discovered the Minoan palace of Knossos.

The Minoans develop a literary system known as the Liner A. They also made great advances in the sciences, arts, construction, ceramics, ship building, and warfare. Ancient historians, Thucydides being among them, credited King Minos for being the first to set up a navy with which he then used to invade or colonized the Cyclades.

Fall of the Minoan Civilization
In accord with geological and archaeological findings on Crete, the fall of this civilization is mainly attributed to the over cultivation of the land which caused deforestation. Nevertheless, it is traditionally accepted that the Minoans were invaded and colonized by the Mycenaeans. The final grounds for the fall of the Minoans is generally acknowledged to be the volcanic eruption near the island of Thera (modern day Santorini) between 1650 and 1550 BC and the ensuing tsunami. As a consequence the isle of Crete was subsumed in water and the cities and villages were demolished. This occasion is often cited as the inspiration of Plato in his mythical work of Atlantis in the dialogues of the *Critias* and *Timaeus*.

Mycenaean Civilization— 1900- 1100
Believed to be the dawn of Greek Culture, the Mycenaean Civilization lasted from around 1900 to1100 BC. The Mycenaeans were credited for instituting the culture mainly due to their advances and enhancement in

architecture, literary system (Liner B, a primitive form of Greek) and religious rites.

Apparently the Minoans of Crete have largely influenced the worship of Mycenaeans. This later culminated to the worship of the ancient Greek Gods.

Fall of Mycenaean Civilization
The major Mycenaean cities in the southwest of Greece were deserted and their civilization annihilated by 1100 BC. Around 1050 BC, the decipherable characteristics of Mycenaean culture had disappeared. The collapse of the Mycenaean civilization is mainly attributed to an environmental calamity combined with the invasion of Doric Greeks.

Greek Dark Age— 1100- 800 BC
Little account exists of the Greek Dark Age, but it is believed to have existed between the fall of the Mycenaean civilization (1100 BC) and the Greek Archaic Period (800 BC).

Life in the Dark Ages for the Greeks was unequivocally challenging. The period saw the abandonment of the old major habitations and the dwindling of the population.

Within these 300 years, the population of Greece dwelled in small nomadic groups; there were no literary relics found which often led to the deduction that they were illiterate. But the Greek began to write yet again in the latter days of the Dark Ages. However, this time they used Linear B script which was used by the Mycenaeans, who implemented the Phoenician alphabet.

Most of the information from the Greek Dark Ages stems from the burial sites and the grave goods contained within them.

Recovery of the Dark Ages and Transition to the Archaic Period

The number of settlements began to increaseby 800 BC. Amongst the changes that were chronicled in the end of the Dark Age were: the revival of literacy (Greek alphabet), the advent of political establishment (the early poleis), and the rise foreign relations beyond the borders of Aegean.

This recovery period signaled the conclusion of the Greek Dark Age and ushered in the Greek Archaic Period— a landmark in the history of Greece.

CHAPTER II

Archaic Greece

Preceded by the Greek Dark Age (1100- 800 BC) and succeeded by the Classical Period (500-323 BC), the Greek Archaic Period lasted from 800 to 500 BC.

The Archaic Period was the epoch that ushered in the Republics, supplanting the Monarchies. It was also the period that bore the institution of laws (Draco's reforms in Athens), pottery and sculpture peculiar to Greece and the minting of the first coins. The great Panathenaeic Festival was also instituted. All these laudable developments paved the way for the emergence and the glory of the Classical Period of Greece.

During the Archaic Period the Greek language, art, architecture, society and politics underwent great changes. These evolutions manifested owing to the incrementing Greek population and commerce. As a result, this introduced the culture of colony and innovative thinking, amongst the most prevalent being Democracy.

Politics & Law

Athens' politics underwent a succession of critical evolutions throughout the archaic period. The first of those changes, however, was rather for the worst—the laws of

Draco (622 or 621 BC). The Athenian legislator's codification was notorious for its severity. Aristotle stated that there wasn't any oddity about Draco's laws worth mentioning *"except their severity in imposing heavy punishment."*

The most austere of all punishments of the time, however, was the death penalty— imposed even for trivial crimes. Plutarch narrates that *"it is said that Draco himself, when asked why he had fixed the punishment of death for most offences, answered that he considered these lesser crimes to deserve it, and he had no greater punishment for more important ones"*. Stating the banal features of the laws, Aristotle maintains that the most important aspect was that the laws were put in writing for the general public for the first time in Athens.

Solon

The key changes that were later introduced to the political sphere were brought about by Solon (594 BC). An Athenian lawmaker and statesman, Solon also enjoyed writing poetry, as patriotic cant, and in the dogged support of the constitutional reforms he made. He is most recognized for reforming the code of laws established by Draco and credited for laying the grounds for the Athenian democracy. The revisions he made bestowed a fair chance to the lower classes— nevertheless, political power was only accessible to the wealthy.

Solon tackled the consequences of disparity, but not their cause. Amongst his reformations the most distinguished was the implementation of the *seisachtheia,* the 'shaking-off-of-burdens". This ruling cancelled debts, forbade the utilization of one's own person as a liability for loan, and summoned back those who had been sold as slaves and those who had fled to evade such fate.

The principles of weights and measures were altered. Among other advancements, the right of third party appeal was established. According to Diogenes Laërtius, in 594 BC, Solon was appointed archon or chief magistrate. He discussed with some of his friends about his planned reforms as an archon. Putting in consideration these new reforms of debt cancelation, these friends instantly took out loans and purchased some land. This new rule, Solon practiced himself; he also exempted his own friends from paying their debts.

This political and constitutional change came fast, and the era of despots that was instigated by Draco soon came to an end.

The Result of Solon's Reform
After Solon finished his reforms, he left Athens for a decade to avoid the pressure of repealing any of his law. According to Herodotus, the nation was obliged to uphold Solon's reform for a decade. Plutarch and the author of the

Athenian Constitution (supposedly Aristotle), on the other hand, maintain that the contracted time was a hundred years. Herodotus' account of the time-span is considered historically accurate by modern scholars for it conforms to the decade long absence of Solon from the nation.

Solon's first travel took him to Egypt. There, he visited the Pharaoh of Egypt Amasis II and wrote political poems. Plutarch states that during Solon's stay, he met with Psenophis of Heliopolis and Sonchis of Sais, two Egyptian priests. Cyprus was his next stop; here he supervised the building of a new capital for the region's king—the indebted king later titled the city Soloi after Solon.

The travels of Solon finally took him to the capital of Lydia, Sardis. This expedition made Solon meet with the Lydian king, Croesus, where he bestowed him an advice, which the king failed to value until it was too late. The story goes as such:

Croesus believed that he was the most blissful soul alive; Solon, however, advised him "*Count no man happy until he be dead*," (which meant that at any minute, there might be a turn of fortune on any one, even the happiest man on earth to make his life insufferable). Croesus understood the depth of Solon's advice when he lost his kingdom to the Persian king Cyrus.

In the four-years Solon was gone, the old social rift re-emerged with unique complications. The procedures the government carried out had some irregularities; elected officials were reluctant to resign and essential posts were regularly left vacant. It has also been argued that people held Solon responsible for the troubles they were encountering.

Finally, Peisistratos, one of Solon's relatives, crushed this dissentient group by force, thereby establishing tyranny without constitutional basis. Plutarch records that Solon held the Athenians responsible for the anarchy and accused them of stupidity and cowardice.

After his return to Athens Solon became a devout opponent of Peisistratos. He, nonetheless, died in Cyprus shortly after at the age of 80 (adhering to his will, his ashes were scattered around Salamis—his birth place).

Economic Reform

Solon has been credited for specific economic reforms and they are:

- Tradesmen from foreign nations were heartened to settle in Athens and those who did were instantly granted citizenship, if they agreed to bring their families with them.
- Fathers were obliged to seek trading opportunities for their sons. Failure to conform to these rules

- resulted in the exemption of the son from taking care of the father when he is old and fragile.
- The Athenian business was encouraged to compete through reformations of measures and weights, perhaps on the strength of prosperous standards.
- The cultivation of olive was promoted; the export of other harvest was banned.

It is generally considered that Solon also was responsible for the reformation of the Athenian coinage. Nevertheless, according to recent studies, it was more likely for Athens to not have coinage at that time until 560 BC, well after Solon's reforms. Early on in the sixth century, the Athenians used silver as a form of payment.

The economic reformation Solon made prompted foreign trade. There was an increasing exportation of the Athenian black-figure pottery between 600 BC and 560 BC. It is believed that the prohibition of exporting grain was a measure to relieve the poor from further predicaments and to secure their benefit.

The promulgation of cultivating olive for export, nonetheless, might have generated more adversity for the majority of Athenians so much so that there was a tremendous decline in the cultivation of land for grain. Furthermore, an olive does not produce fruit for six years.

Poetry

Solon is one of the Athenian poets whose work has endures to this day. We could find Solons verses in the fragmented quotations of Demosthenes, Plutarch and many others who had employed them to support their arguments. Some of the fragments may have been erroneously accredited to him and some interpolations may have also been spotted by some experts. Solon was also one of the first citizens of Athens to reference the goddess Athena.

Most of his enduring verses illustrate him as a political activist bent on asserting personal authority and leadership. The German classicist Wilamowitz described his writing as a "versified harangue". Plutarch, nevertheless, states that Solon initially wrote poetry for enjoyment, dilating on pleasure in a rather popular fashion.

His elegiac approach is purported to have the stamps of Tyrtaeus. According to one historian, his iambic and trochaic verses were more direct and energetic than his elegies and perhaps set the stage for the iambics of Athenian drama.

The Peisistratids

The Athenian tyrants that started with Peisistratos were known as the Peisistratids. The term 'tyrant' didn't contain the negative implications it has today. In truth, Peisistratos didn't have the characteristics of a draconian ruler, as he felt sympathy towards the commoners of Athens to some extent.

Until the assassination plot of Harmodios and Aristogeiton, Hippias and Hipparchos, sons of Peisistratos, carried on with the tyranny. Cleisthenes ascended to power in the political gap that followed the tyrannicides. He is accredited for the introduction of *isonomia* (equal laws) in Athens. He was able to achieve this through various reforms, which undermined the prominence of the aristocrats. The tribal system of Athens was one of the major reforms that Cleisthenes implemented.

Prior to the reforms he made, there existed four tribes which were based on family ties. Cleisthenes altered these to ten tribes, each structured by a rater intricate subsystem.

Panhellenic Games

The Panhellenic games of Greece were founded during the Archaic period. It was around 776 BC that Hercules and Pelops began the Olympic Games— the classical Temple of Zeus exhibits their influence. Delphi, a city also known as the home of the Pythian Games, hosted several athletic games from 586 BC. At Corinth in 581 BC, the Panhellenic Isthmian Games were founded and in 573 BC the Nemean games were originated.

These games were, however, imbued with mythical sentiments and not just the Olympics. According to Pindar, the Pythian Games, which had initially been only a game of dance and music, were purportedly founded by Apollo; the Isthmian Games, according to Pausanias, by the King of Corinth, Sisyphus; and the Nemean Games, after the Nemean lion was slain by Hercules.

Art & Architecture

There were major advances in the realm of art and architecture during this period. Orientalizing style supplanted the earlier geometric style; it was in turn replaced by black figure pottery. Black figure pottery was initially started to be employed in Corinth, 700s BC, historians, however, argue that it dates back to 570 BC; and its successor, the Red Figure style, developed in about 530 BC.

During this period a plethora of advances were made to the building of temples. The primary stage of the Heraion at Samos was constructed in the middle of the 8th century BC; it was only until 530 BC that its final, incomplete, reincarnation began.

The Lelantine War— 710-650 BC

The Lelantine War was a vicious battle that occurred in Euboea in the Archaic Period, The conflict was between Chalcis and Eretria—ancient Greek states. It was the earliest Greek war (after the mythical Trojan War) that had any claim to be considered "general," in a sense that it engaged distant allies on each side.

"The war between Chalcis and Eretria was the one in which most cities belonging to the rest of Greece were divided up into alliances with one side or the other."

— Thucydides

According to tradition, the ground to this war, which was around 710-650 BC, was the fight for Lelantine Plain in Euboea.

As the ports of Euboea, both Chalcis and Eretria claimed the rights to the Lelantine Plain. Although Eretria is situated outside the land, it had historical claims to it. One probable reason for this would be that Eretria was originally the harbor of a mother town located further east. That town was situated at the entrance of the Lelas, near modern Lefkandi. Lefkandi underwent very difficult destructions in 825 BC, after which the influx of its population moved to Eretria.

The origin of the War

For a large period of time, this fertile land had been employed for agricultural purposes— mainly for vine cultivation. Due to the scarcity of fertile land in Greece, wars for agriculturally alluring landscape were not peculiar, especially during the Archaic period, an example would be the war between Megara and Athens. It is amorphous though, why Chalcis and Eretria abruptly engaged in a dispute over the Lelantine Plain after being in harmony on its long term use.

Natural disasters could also be held accountable for causing the war. In the late 8th century BC, Euboea, Attica, and other adjacent islands underwent severe drought; and as a result, Eretrian settlements on Andros was deserted. The drought and the following famine may have led both Eretria and Chalcis to claim rights to the Lelantine Plain.

The war between Chalcis and Eretria is usually dated to 710 BC. Though both cities possessed large fleets, the war was waged on land. The majority of the combatants then were perhaps not heavily armed swordsmen, since the war preceded the advent of hoplite warfare. According to another source, the war mainly involved cavalry engagements.

The battle primarily involved the two cities and their territories. During the war, Eretria comprised a quarter of the islands of Euboea and the nearby Cyclades (Kea, Tenos and Andros). Accounts regarding the extent of the conflict and the amount of allies are contentious. There are direct mentions of a triad of participants: Samos as well as Thessaly (on that of Chalcis) and Miletus (on the side of Eretria).

The mother town of Eretria at Lefkandi around 700 BC was finally destroyed (most probably by Chalcis), cutting Eretria's link to the Lelantine Plain. Around this time, Miletus, Eretria's ally, raided the town of Karystos, aspiring to be the central power in the eastern region of Aegean. The war endured till the middle of the 7th century BC and Chalcis ended up being the nominal victor.

The era also saw the advance of the Greek alphabet through Phoenicia, which may be indicative of the importance of trade developments.

The aftermath of the war on the defeated Eretria and the assumed victor Chalcis was severe – the warring parties lost their former political and economic prominence.

Eretria supported Miletus during the Ionian Revolt, as a way to repay Miletus for helping it in the Lelantine war.

CHAPTER III

Classical Greece

Classical Greece emerged right after the Archaic Period came to a conclusion. And for about 200 years thereafter, Greece enjoyed a period of unparalleled prominence and prosperity.

During the Classical period, Greece reached the summit of its glory and took the world by its breath. It was the time in which modern thinking, art, literature, science and philosophy began to take their first steps; it was when democracy literary took its first breath; the Classical era was the extraordinary period that gave life to the greatest thinkers of our world – Socrates, Plato, Aristotle where but a few.

But the Classical era wasn't just about prosperity for Greece; it was also a time where conflict, turmoil and devastation inundated the inhabitants of this grand empire.

The Rise of Classical Greece

Classical Greece was born out of conflict and raised to the highest level of prosperity. The beginning of this phenomenal era is a rather controversial matter. Some historians say that it rose around 480 BC when the Greeks finally defeated the Persians at the Battle of Salamis.

Defeating the Persian Empire was a great challenge for the Greeks. To halt the invasion of this mighty force and secure their sovereignty, the Greeks had to set aside their differences and unite. And with this unity, which was the most powerful weapon the Greeks had, victory was attained. The Athenians and Spartans were the most powerful forces during the Persian Wars.

After the war, Athens then established a defense alliance with other Greek city states to prevent future invasion attempts of the Persians. The league was called Delian League; it was named after the island on which its treasury was kept, Delos.

And as the host and head of the Delian Legue, Athens demanded tribute from other Greek states. With all this power and control, Athens then became a superpower, with a navy to be reckoned with, and notable growth in the political, economical and cultural arena.

These were the chronicled events that marshaled in the Classical era. According to other historians, however, what marked the beginning of Classical Greece was the fall of the last Athenian tyrant, Hippias (son of Peisistratos), and the proclamation of Cleisthenes' reform.

In 508 BC, Cleisthenes, a noble Athenian from the Alcmaeonid family, managed to oust the Athenian tyrant Hippias and rise to power. He then established a democratic government and gave the Classical era an eternal spot in world history.

Cleisthenes instituted a new administrative system called Demokratia, meaning Democracy or 'Power of the People'. This administration allowed for civilians aged above eighteen to exercise their power by taking part in the ekklesia (The Assembly). The ekklesia was chaired by a council of 500 sporadically selected individuals. All officials were sworn to act *'according to the laws, what is best for the people'*.

To create political diversity, the new government also divided the city of Athens in to thirty trittyes:

- Ten trittyes in Paralie, the coastal
- Ten trittyes in Asty, the urban centre
- Ten trittyes Mesogia, in rural

Because of this constitutional reform, which humanity still abides by, Cleisthenes and the hub of modern civilization, Greece, is known and adulated as 'The Father of Democracy'.

"Our polity does not copy the laws of neighboring states; we are rather a pattern to others than imitators ourselves. It is called a democracy, because not the few but the many govern. If we look to the laws, they afford equal justice to all in their private differences; if to social standing,

advancement in public life falls to reputation for capacity, class considerations not being allowed to interfere with merit; nor again does poverty bar the way, if a man is able to serve the state, he is not hindered by the obscurity of his condition."

Thucydides, Pericles' Funeral Oration'.

Athens under Pericles

Pericles, whose name also means 'surrounded by glory', was one of Greeks greatest statesman. He was also a famous orator, a patron of art, literature, and an extraordinary general that marshaled in the Athenian Golden Age.

He had the greatest influence in Athens, so much so that even the renowned historian, Thucydides, referred to him as 'The first citizen of Athens'.

Pericles was born into a powerful and noble family, in 495 BC His father, Xanthippus, was one of the greatest heroes in the Persian War and his mother, Agariste, hailed from the wealthy and noble Alcmaeonidae family.

He spent most of his early years avoiding public appearance and focusing more on his studies, music, art, literature and philosophy. He surrounded himself with the era's greatest thinkers and became close friends with most of them, as in Anaxagoras, Zeno of Elea, and Protagoras.

Pericles entered the political arena in 470 BC. But his grand presence wasn't consolidated until 463 BC when he became the leading prosecutor of Cimon, a political leader accused of treason, and managed to successfully ostracize him.

Then in 461 BC following the exile of Cimon, he presided over Athens' Democratic Party. Pericles propagated a populist social policy. And highlighting this stand of his, the first decree he proposed was the free admission of the poor in theatrical plays. And from 458 – 457 BC he started giving out generous wages for all citizens serving as jurymen in the Heliaia (the supreme court of Athens), and he lessened the property requisites for the archonship.

Pericles also issued certain constitutions that had him face a heap of criticism. For instance, in 451 BC he set limitations on Athenian citizenship on those who didn't have Athenian parentage on both sides.

"Rather, the admiration of the present and succeeding ages will be ours, since we have not left our power without witness, but have shown it by mighty proofs; and far from needing a Homer for our panegyrist, or other of his craft whose verses might charm for the moment only for the impression which they gave to melt at the touch of fact, we have forced every sea and land to be the highway of our

daring, and everywhere, whether for evil or for good, have left imperishable monuments behind us."

Thucydides, Pericles' Funeral Oration'.

Then in 454 BC Pericles chronicled one of his greatest accomplishments; he led a successful military campaign in Corinth and established Athenian colonies in Thrace and on the Black Sea coast.

Pericles then reached the summit of his political career when he became an elected General or a Strategos, in 443 BC.

The Athenian Golden Age and Pericles

The years of the Athenian Golden Age is normally set between the end of the Persian war and the beginning of the Peloponnesian War. Several sources, however, refer to the Golden Age of Athens as a period that took place during the ruling days of Pericles.

As earlier stated, the assets of the confederacy of allies, the Delian League, was based in Delos. But then in 454 BC, after a failed attack on the Persians in Egypt, Athenian officials decided to transfer the League's treasury from Delos to Athens.

Then during the mid 440 BC, Pericles began to extort the League's treasury and fund the construction of several projects in Athens.

The buildings on the acropolis of Athens – the Athena Nike, the Erechtheum and the mighty Parthenon— were the most notable and the ones that marked the Golden Age of Athens. Following the completion of these projects, Pericles delivered his celebrated acclamation for veterans who died in defense of Greece at the Battle of Marathon.

"Remember, too, that if your country has the greatest name in all the world, it is because she never bent before disaster; because she has expended more life and effort in war than any other city, and has won for herself a power greater than any hitherto known, the memory of which will descend to the latest posterity."

Thucydides,Pericles' Third Oration'

For these projects, the greatest engineers, architects and artists in Greece were put to work.

He also funded the reconstruction of certain parts of Athens that were destroyed during the Persian Wars, which included the temple at Hephaestos, the Odeion concert hall, and the temple of Poseidon at Attica.

The strengthening of democracy was also a prime priority for this leader. He used these funds to pay generous wages to jurymen and members of the Ekklesia (Athenian assembly) to enable more civic participation.

Art and Philosophy in Classical Greece

Art, philosophy and architecture blossomed in Greece during the ruling days of Pericles.

From childhood, Pericles was a huge fan and advocate of art and philosophy. And when he got the unlimited access to the League's treasury, almost instantly he leaped on to becoming a patron of the Arts.

He funded the annual production of dramatic and comedic plays at the Acropolis, which gave way for the world's greatest writers like Aeschylus, Sophocles, Aristophanes, and Euripides to flourish.

Sculptors like Phidias found the opportunity to create masterpieces such as the statue of the renowned Zeus at Olympia and the statue of the goddess Athena for the Parthenon.

The master of marble and stone, Myron, structured the Discus Thrower. Hippocrates, 'the Father of Medicine', began his practice. Historians such as Herodotus and Thucydides rose to glory.

As evidenced by the teaching of the world's greatest thinkers such as Socrates, Plato and other sophists such as Protagoras, philosophy, which means 'love of wisdom', also set its roots during this period.

Many more phenomenal creations and events took place during this time.

The Peloponnesian War

Under Pericles' leadership, Athens self-evidently reached the summit of her glory. At the same time, however, Sparta along with other city states from the Peloponnesus region felt threatened by the growing power of the Athenian hegemony of Greece and thus established an alliance of their own called the Peloponnesian League.

In time, the suspicion, envy and animosity of the two powers then grew larger than expected and it wasn't long before it reached a stage of eruption and resulted in the epic conflict called the Peloponnesian War in 431 BC.

Who or what instigated the war is still a debatable matter. And as the Athenians have more account of the war than the Spartans or other Greek city states, it's a challenge to verify anything.

According to historians, the conflict began when the Spartans demanded concessions from the Athenians. Pericles refused their demand and the war commenced.

Other historians, however, believe that it was the Athenian siege of Potidaea and the economic sanction, 'Megarian Decrees', Athens decreed upon the Megarian people that triggered the war.

Athens was then accused of violating the Thirty Years Peace by the Peloponnesian League. And war was soon declared.

For the first two years, Pericles oversaw the army of Athens. But then, in the summer of 430 BC, while he was in a naval expedition to raze Peloponnese's coasts, a callous plague broke out in the city of Athens and devastated the lives of many people.

In the autumn of 429 BC Pericles, along with his family died out of this epidemic.

> *"For heroes have the whole earth for their tomb; and in lands far from their own, where the column with its epitaph declares it, there is enshrined in every breast a record unwritten with no tablet to preserve it, except that of the heart."*
>
> Thucydides, Pericles' Funeral Oration'.

Pericles' overall leadership and performance in the war was heavily criticized. Some historians such Thucydides, have defended his name by saying such things as, "he kept himself untainted by corruption, although he was not altogether indifferent to money-making".

And others like Plato and Plutarch didn't shy away from denouncing him:

"As I know, Pericles made the Athenians slothful, garrulous and avaricious, by starting the system of public fees"

– Plato.

"He was no longer the same man as before, nor alike submissive to the people and ready to yield and give in to the desires of the multitude as a steersman to the breezes…… Many others say that the people were first led on by him into allotments of public lands, festival-grants, and distributions of fees for public services, thereby falling into bad habits, and becoming luxurious and wanton under the influence of his public measures, instead of frugal and self-sufficing"

– Plutarch.

Athens was nevertheless weakened by the plague and Pericles' death. According to Thucydides' recordings, the leaders that followed lacked a great deal of competence. They were, as he said *"committing even the conduct of state affairs to the whims of the multitude"*.

The compatible strength of both forces perpetuated the war; Athens with a naval power and Sparta with a strong land-based military power. Then in 421 BC the Athenian leader Nicias initiated a treaty with Sparta, the Peace of Nicias, which only lasted until 418 BC.

Athens struggled throughout the war, and in some instances, did manage to survive. But after a dreadful defeat in Sicily in 413 BC, it was impossible for Athens to resurrect.

The Peloponnesian War lasted for almost thirty years. And it ended in 404 BC with Sparta coming out the victor.

The end of Classical Greece

After the Peloponnesian War, Classical Greece began to march towards its end. With an enfeebled naval power and lost political supremacy, Athens was left in ruins and was forced to bid her glory days, farewell.Historians often refer to this period as the Late Classical Era.

Sparta then became a superpower and sustained that position for about thirty year. But the Peloponnesian War wasn't the last conflict Sparta had to face. There was also another rival that threatened the welfare of this great city state – Thebes.

The long and arduous war with Thebes drove Sparta to bankruptcy, which led to its downfall.

The fragmented condition of the Athenian Empire and the weakening of Sparta and Thebes, paved the way for the Macedonian King Philip II to conquer Greece in 338 BC.

The Greeks considered the Macedonians as barbarians or 'barbaros' meaning 'foreign'. And to prevent their invasion, the Greeks yet again agreed to set their differences aside, unite and fight this new force with might and main. But Philip II was a force to be reckoned with. After a successful win at the Battle of Chaeronea, the Greek forces subsided and he asserted his authority.

In the following years, Philip II managed to unite the whole of Greece and station it under Macedonian rule.

Then in 336 BC Philip was assassinated and his son Alexander the Great acceded to the throne.

Alexander the Great
Alexander the Great acceded to the throne right after his father was assassinated. He was the brave ruler that expanded the frontiers of Greece; his conquests included

Egypt, Persia, Asia Minor, India and so forth. It was his military might that earned him the title 'the Great'.

In his youth, he was tutored by one of Greek's greatest philosophers, Aristotle. And wherever he went Alexander made sure that the ideals of Greek civilization, culture, language, art and literature spread.

The end of Classical Greece is marked by the sudden death of Alexander the Great in 323 BC.

CHAPTER IV

Hellenistic Greece

The Hellenistic Period of Greece began in 323 BC following Alexander the Great's death and ended in 31 BC after the invasion of the Roman Republic. The period is characterized by the spread of Greek civilization, thinking, language and mores throughout the whole of the eastern Mediterranean region, and Southwest Asia. The word "Hellenistic" comes from the word Hellazein, which, when translated, means "to speak Greek or identify with the Greeks."

In the wake of Alexander's death there followed a power struggle between his generals (the Diadochoi). They reigned over the Alexandrian empire and frequently fought common enemies as well as one another. The strife culminated to the emergence of three major kingdoms: Syria and the rags of the Empire of Persia were ruled over by Seleucus (Seleucid Empire); Macedonia, Thrace and certain parts of Asia Minor were controlled by Antigonus and his son Demetrius (Antigonid dynasty); Egypt and regions of the Middle East were under the reign of Ptolemy (Ptolemaic Kingdom).

There were also other small kingdoms at the time; the Attalid kingdom and the kingdom of Bactria were amongst the few.

The Hellenistic era saw the rise of cities. Athens, Thebes, Miletus, Corinth, and Syracuse were among the Greek cities that saw great prosperity. Outside the realm of Greece, cities likeEphesus, Pergamum, Damascus, Antioch and Trapezus also rose to prominence. However, the city of Alexandria towered over all of them. Founded by Alexander in 331 BC, the city became the epicenter of trade and the culture of the Hellenistic world.

The era boasted a host of celebrated thinkers and artists whose works continued to influence the world for centuries. Greece's philosophical culture was maintained through schools of thoughts such as the Skeptics, Epicurians and Stoics. Works of literature, art and poetry reached their zenith. The works of Theocritos, Kalimachus, Menander and Apollonious of Rhodes attest to the era's innovative growth in artistry.

The growth was facilitated by the great kings of Greece. They commissioned the works of art, sculpture and jewelry, built large, ornate buildings and even made massive donations for the construction of zoos, museums, universities and libraries (the celebrated libraries at Alexandria and Pergamon, for instance).Mathematicians like Euclid, Archimedes and Apollonios, along with the inventors Heron (engineer of the model steam engine) Ktesibios (creator of the water clock) hail from the University of Alexandria that was established through the sponsoring of the Greek kings.

The kings were also cosmopolitan thinkers who worked tirelessly to collect the world's riches. They promoted trade relationships throughout the Hellenistic world. From India, they imported ebony, pearls, ivory, cotton, gold, spices and sugar; from the Far East, iron and fur; from Babylon and Damascus, prunes and dates; olive oil from the city of Athens; silver from Spain; and from islands as far north as Cornwall and Brittany, they imported tin.

But the Hellenistic era was far from perfect. The kingdoms were plagued by external and internal unrest. The continued struggle between the major and minor kingdoms led to the constant realignment of boarders. The large extent of the empire's territory led to an unwieldy system of control; this gave way to foreign attacks, especially in the areas outside the large cities. These areas became easy targets of piracy and robbery.

The most serious threat to the empire came in 279 BC, when Macedonia was invaded by the Gauls in an attempt to steal the treasure of Delphi. Ptolemy II, who was the self-asserted king of Macedonia at the time, was killed during the invasion. He was beheaded and the enemy had his head attached to the tip of a sphere. His death led to the region's disorder. However, Antigonus II Gonatas was able to nib this incursion in the bud. In 277 BC, he was able to crush a force of 18,000 Gauls. He later appointed himself king of Macedonia and ruled for over three decades.

The wars of the Diadochi

A debate over the future of the Alexandrian empire arose amongst the Diadochis ('successors'; the title given to the first generation of political and military leaders after the death of Alexander). Some supported the unification of the kingdom, whilst others argued for its fragmentation.

The debate culminated to the Wars of the Diadochi (321-301). There were four wars that took place: The First Diadochi War (321-320); The Second Diodochi War (318-316); The Third Diadochi War (315-311) and The Fourth Diodochi War (307-301).

The Diadochi Wars were concluded with the disintegration of the empire and the allocation of its territories in Asia and Europe to the commanders. The highlight of the settlement at Triparadisuswas the following:

Egypt fell under the provincial rule of Ptolemy; Seleucus was granted Babylonia; Lysimachus kept Thrace; Antigenes, was granted Elam; Arridaeus, a former regent, became the satrap of Hellespontine Phrygia; Peithon, got Media and Antigonus was given control over the army of Perdiccas.

The new regent became Antipater—Alexander's leading general. He was given the responsibility of sheltering the young Alexander IV, Philip Arridaeus and the queen Roxane.

The Ptolemaic Dynasty

Following the death of Alexander the Great, Perdiccas ruled the empire as the regent of the joint kings Alexander IV (Alexander's infant child) and Philip III of Macedonia (Alexander's half –brother). Ptolemy was appointed by Perdiccas as the provincial governor of Egypt.

When the Alexandrian empire descended into chaos, Ptolemy asserted himself as ruler of Egypt; During the Wars of the Diadochi (322-301), he successfully overcame the invasion of Perdiccas in 321 BC and strengthened his reign in Egypt and the surrounding regions, namely Coele-Syria, Cyprus and Libya.

In 305 BC Ptolemy became king of Egypt and founded the Ptolemaic dynasty. He was titled Ptolemy I Soter (meaning 'savior'). He earned the epithet Soter because of the support he gave to the Rhodians during the Siege of Rhodes. The capital city of the kingdom became Alexandria; its territories were far reaching, including today's Libya, Israel, Palestine, Turkey, Cyprus, Lebanon, Jordan and Syria. The kingdom ruled until 30 BC.

All his male successors took the name 'Ptolemy', and the women took the names Cleopatra, Arsinoe and Berenice. The Ptolemies respected the Egyptian culture and religion. The Egyptians, however begrudgingly, accepted them as the successors of the pharaohs. However, their political system favored the Greco-Macedonian elites who were often granted exclusive privileges.

The Ptolemies were also quick to adapt the tradition of the pharaohs; this was reflected in their wardrobe, their practice of incestuous and their participation in the religion of the Egyptians. They also commissioned the building of temples for the Egyptian gods.

The leaders were great patrons of the arts and innovative thinking; they established libraries and sponsored scientific researches and individual scholars. During the reign of Ptolemy II, great poets such as Theocritus, Apollonius of Rhodes and Callimachus (the keeper of the Library of Alexandria) transformed Alexandria into the hub of Hellenistic literature.

The Ptolemaic kings fought with the Seleucids for years over the territory of Coele-Syria; these wars were called the 'Syrian Wars'.

The most celebrated Ptolemaic monarchy was Cleopatra VII, who was known for her lustrous affairs with the Roma Republic's Caesar and his cousin Mark Anthony. Her participation in the Battle of Actium also adds to her fame.

The Empire of Seleucid

The Seleucid Empire (312-363 BC) was founded by Seleucus I Nicator in the year he asserted himself ruler of Babylon; initially he was the provincial governor of Babylon appointed by the regent Perdiccas whom he later helped assassin. He continued to expand his territory in to the near east domain of the Alexandrian Empire. During the peak of the empire, its dominion included today's Armenia, Georgia, India, Iran, Israel, Kuwait, Kazakhstan, Palestine and many more.

> *"Always lying in wait for the neighboring nations, strong in arms and persuasive in council, he [Seleucus] acquired Mesopotamia, Armenia, 'Seleucid' Cappadocia, Persis, Parthia, Bactria, Arabia, Tapouria, Sogdia, Arachosia, Hyrcania, and other adjacent peoples that had been subdued by Alexander, as far as the river Indus, so that the boundaries of his empire were the most extensive in Asia after that of Alexander. The whole region from Phrygia to the Indus was subject to Seleucus"* —Appain, The Syrian Wars.

Like the Ptolemaic dynasty, there remained a Greco-political elite that was strengthened by the emigration from Greece. The capital of the Empire was Antioch where the Hellenistic culture flourished.

Following the death of Seleucus, the kingdom became fraught with problems. His successors Antiochos I, Antiochos II, Seleucos II and Seleucos III were faced with a legion of battles including the revolt of Parthia,

Bythinia, Pergammum and Bactria. They also had to deal with the First Syrian war that the kingdom fought with the Ptolemaic Kingdom. Intra-fighting also contributed to the dynasty's decay.

Antiochos III ascended to the throne in 223 BCE, inheriting the ruins of the empire. At the tender age of eighteen, he managed to quell the uprising of the states and restore stability in the empire.

His momentous battles had him collide with the strengthening Roman Republic when he expanded his territory to Anatolia. He was defeated by the Romans at the Battle of Magnesia ad Sipylum in 190 BC.

The peace treaty signed after the conclusion of the war had devastating consequences. It had the kingdom reach its nadir; from which it was never to recover.

After the death of Antiochos III in 187 BC, the kingdom fell prey to dynastic struggles and rebellions. It remained in tatters until its final demise caused by the growing powers of Rome and Parthia.

CHAPTER V

The Fall of Ancient Greece

Ancient Greece fell as a result of gradual erosion that was brought about by the towering influence of the Roman Republic.

Despite the constant resistance of the kingdoms, Greece, overpowered by the rising influence of the republic, progressively succeeded its territories. The Battle of Actium in 31 BC signaled the conclusion of the Hellenistic era and thus Ancient Greece.

First Roman-Greek Collision

During the Hellenistic age the Roman Republic was beginning to rise to prominence. The Roman-Greek clashes commenced when the Roman Republic invaded a Greek colony in the Italian peninsula. The confrontation led to a naval warfare after which the Greek colonies appealed to Pyrrhus, the king of Epirus, for military support. Pyrrhus responded by sending a troop of 25,000 men in Italy in 280 BC.

Pyrrhus, understanding that he was situated in a rather unpropitious position, withdrew from Italy. The two warring parties met again in 275 BC at the Battle of Beneventum. The triumphant party was undetermined, but

Pyrrhus withdrew again when learning that his crew had been fatigued and diminished by years of foreign wars.

This war was a decisive event that emboldened the Roman Republic. One of the unparalleled forces in the Mediterranean basin was challenged by this young yet threatening force. Now Rome was off to challenge the other superpower—the Carthaginian Kingdom.

Shortly after the Battle of Beneventum, Rome fell foul with the Carthaginian Kingdom over the island of Sicily. This led to the First Punic War (264–241 BC). Rome defeated Carthage, retaining full control over the island. The republic then continued to supplant Greek rule in the Italian peninsula and gained full domination over the peninsula.

First Macedonian War

Pirate attacks of Roman merchants in Illyria, drew the attention of the Roman Republic to the Balkans. Following the first and second Illyrian Wars, the republic invaded the region.

It was when the Macedonian king Philip V offered one of the major pirates Demetrius of Pharos refuge that tension between Rome and Macedonia arose. And it was in the course of the Second Punic War (218–201 BC) Philip V allied with Carthage to weaken the influence of Rome in the Balkans. At the time, Hannibal (of Carthage) had managed to strike a hard blow on the Romans at the Battle of Cannae (216 BC). Its army was depleted when Philip V declared war.

The war came to be known as the First Macedonian War (215–202 BC). Besides asserting Philip V as Rome's arch nemesis, the war yielded no real results.

Second Macedonian War

The Roman Republic emerged as the victor in the Second Punic War. After the restoration of its army's strength, the republic set out to assert its authority in the Balkans and undercut the spread of Philip V's influence in the region. Rome waged war on Macedonia in 200 BC and also made allies with Philip V's enemies, the Aetolian League of Greek city-states.

Rome defeated Philip V in the Battle of Cynoscephalae (197 BC); the republic subjected his kingdom to a devastating indemnity, and confiscated his fleet. This signaled the conclusion of Macedonia's preeminent rule in the Mediterranean.

Roman-Syrian War

The defeat of Macedonia left the Seleucid Empire in great bewilderment. This was because in 203 BC the Seleucid

Antiochus III had joined forces with Philip V. The two forces were in cahoots to overthrow Ptolemy V, the boy-king of Egypt.

Antiochus III managed to defeat Ptolemy in the Fifth Syrian War and forged ahead in pursuit of possessing the Ptolemaic territory in Asia Minor. This endeavor brought him in conflict with the Roman allies in the region—Rhodes and Pergamum. Eventually, this led to a cold war between Antiochus III and the Roman Republic.

On the other front, the earlier allies of Rome, the Aetolian League, which had helped bring Philip V to his defeat, began to resent the presence of the Romans in Greece. To Antiochus III this was the perfect window. Under the pretext of 'liberating Greece from the influence of Rome' he invaded Greece. This commenced the Roman-Syrian War (192–188 BC).

The Romans were able to trounce the army of Antiochus III and thus bring another Greek kingdom to its demise.

Third Macedonian War

The Macedonian kings could be held responsible for the empire's colossal failure. It was their inordinate ambition and their inadvertent provocation of Rome that gave way to the Republic's dominance.

The Third Macedonian War (171–168 BC) was initiated by Perseus (the son of Philip V) who had hoped to reaffirm the power of Macedonian and the autonomy of Greece. Rome not only came out the victor in this battle but also ousted the kingdom of Macedonia and replaced it with four puppet republics.

Macedonia remained under their reign for two decades until its final annexation to the Roman Republic in 146 BC.

Mithridatic Wars

The Mithridatic Wars can be seen as the last resistance of the Greeks. In 88 BC, King Mithridates of Pontus marched with his army to Anatolia and murdered 100,000 Roman and Roma allies throughout Asia Minor. Emboldened by his intrepid feat, the Greek cities—Athens included—toppled Roman puppet rulers and participated in the Mithridatic Wars.

Despite the momentous rally of the people of Greece, the rebellion was crushed when in 65 BC Mithridates was eventually trounced by Gnaeus Pompeius Magnus (Pompey the Great).

The cities of Greece were further plagued by the Roman civil wars which had taken place on their land. This not only destroyed the cities but also depopulated and dispirited the population.

The Battle of Actium

The Roman Empire continued to undermine the rags of Ancient Greece, either by supplanting the kingdoms by its puppet republics or depleting the forces of the monarchies. The Greek kingdoms disintegrated as they became vulnerable to the incursions of the tribes hailing from the fringes.

What sounded the knell of ancient Greece was the Battle of Actium, fought between Octavian (later Augustus) and Cleopatra VII, the last Ptolemaic monarch, and her lover Mark Anthony.

In a way this could be seen as the Roman Republic's civil war in that Mark Anthony— a former ally of Octavian— was fighting against the Roman Republic under which he had served throughout his whole life.

In the naval battle of Actium on September 2nd 30 BC, Octavian triumphed, conquering the whole of Egypt. Mark Anthony and Cleopatra withdrew to the city of Alexandria and suicided.

Octavian asserted the demise of both Ancient Greece and the Roman Republic. In 27 BC, he annexed Greece to the Roman Empire; she came to be known as 'the province of Achaea'.

Bonus Chapter

10 Little Known Facts about Ancient Greece

Barbers in Ancient Greece

Today, a barber doesn't have as much prominence as that of a doctor, a scientist or a professor. But in ancient Greece a barber was the esteemed individual that was greeted with a bow.

Yes, barbers in ancient Greece were very important. And that was because Greek men were obsessed with their beards. Just like how we today assert our stand in society by the wardrobes we wear or the cars we drive; Greek men used to parade their beards to turn eyes.

The barbers were quite rich then.

Medicine in Ancient Greece

The torpedo or the electric ray, which is a type of fish that can emit a strong electric discharge from its organs, were put to great use in ancient Greece.

The Greeks used theses fishes, or the electricity they discharge for medical purposes. Much like how in the ER today, doctors use electric shock to revive the pulse of a silenced heart, the Greeks would place the fish on the thorax of a sick person to stimulate the reflexes of vital organs.

The parentage of the toasting culture

Making a toast at weddings, dinner parties, graduations, birthdays is no oddity. It has actually become a world custom now. Ever wonder as to where this renowned tradition came from?

Yes, well don't wander far; it was from the ancient Greeks!

In ancient Greece, it was a custom for the hosts of dinner parties to take the first sip of wine and utter the phrase 'Drinking to one's health'. This was to ensure the guests that the wine wasn't poisoned.

What the Greeks never knew about

Today, oranges, lemons, tomatoes and potatoes are amongst the most heavily consumed vegetables and fruits in the world. In ancient Greece though, not one person had a taste of these delectable plants.

And it wasn't that these vegetable and fruits were forbidden, it was simply because they were unknown at that time. Yes, unknown!

Ancient Greeks used to build pyramids

It so happens that pyramids weren't just an Egyptian thing. Around 500 BC the Greeks used to build pyramids out of porous rocks in arid areas and use them to conserve water.

Experts say that the movement of the wind through the porous stones combined with the alternating temperatures of the day would cause condensation, which is believed to stream down and feed a system of pipes.

Incredible, huh?

The Greeks were the first to build a tunnel

Of course, skillful engineers and tunnels like the channel-tunnel deserve all kinds of adulation. But ancient Greeks also need to be well acclaimed for being the first in the world to build a tunnel.

In the 6th century BC, the Greeks dug a half a mile tunnel on the Aegean island of Samos. The construction began on both ends and the two halves were joined in the middle.

This tunnel was supervised by the renowned Greek architect Eupalinus.

Ancient Greeks and meat

For the majority of society today, life without meat is unimaginable. But for ancient Greeks it meant nothing.

It was forbidden, against all principles and spiritual beliefs, for the Greeks to eat meat. But if the animal has been sacrificed to a god, then indulgence was surly permitted.

Origin of Feta cheese

Feta cheese, which is a dairy product made out of goat and sheep milk, is Greek's national cheese and currently, one of the world's most favored dairy product.

And guess what, its origin dates back to the glorious days of ancient Greece. And that fact is evidenced by the mention of feta cheese in Homer's epic poem 'The Odyssey'.

The Greeks were the first to host the Olympic Games

Yes, it's true. And not much to your surprise, the Greeks weren't just the first in the world to host the Olympic Games but they were also the ones who created it.

Today, the Olympic Games are purposed to promote international goodwill. In ancient Greece though, it had a rather profound religious sentiment. It was a festival held at Olympia, hence the name Olympic Games, in honor of the mighty god Zeus.

It hosted athletic, musical and literary contests and participants hailed from every part of Greece. And just like today's Olympic Games, it was held every four years.

The first Olympic Game in ancient Greece was held in 776 BC and the champion was a Cook named Coroebus who came first in the sprint race.

What great innovators, those Greeks.

Slaves in ancient Greece

In ancient Greece those who were condemned to thralldom were criminals, abandoned children, war prisoners and children of slaves. But what is fascinating about the slaves in ancient Greece was that they constituted 40% – 80% of the population.

Printed in Great Britain
by Amazon